CLASSIC ROCK SHEET MUSIC HITS

Product Line Manager: Carol Cuellar
Project Manager: Zobeida Pérez
Cover Design: Joe Klucar

CONTENTS

HOTEL CALIFORNIA

Words and Music by
DON HENLEY, GLENN FREY and DON FELDER

Hotel California - 7 - 1

6

Hotel California - 7 - 4

8

Hotel California - 7 - 7

AFTER MIDNIGHT

Words and Music by
JOHN J. CALE

Moderate Rock beat, in 2

After mid - night,___ we're gon - na let it all___ hang down.___

After mid - night,___ we're gon - na shake your tam - bou - rine.___

Af - ter

Af - ter

After Midnight - 3 - 1

12

AMERICAN PIE

Words and Music by
DON McLEAN

American Pie - 7 - 1

In a moderate tempo

*See the last page for the lyrics of stanzas 2, 3 and 4.

16

18

American Pie - 7 - 6

2. Now for ten years we've been on our own, and moss grows fat on a rollin' stone
   But that's not how it used to be when the jester sang for the king and queen
   In a coat he borrowed from James Dean and a voice that came from you and me
   Oh and while the king was looking down, the jester stole his thorny crown
   The courtroom was adjourned, no verdict was returned
   And while Lennin read a book on Marx the quartet practiced in the park
   And we sang dirges in the dark
   The day the music died
   We were singin'...bye-bye...etc.

3. Helter-skelter in the summer swelter the birds flew off with a fallout shelter
   Eight miles high and fallin' fast, it landed foul on the grass
   The players tried for a forward pass, with the jester on the sidelines in a cast
   Now the half-time air was sweet perfume while the sergeants played a marching tune
   We all got up to dance but we never got the chance
   'Cause the players tried to take the field, the marching band refused to yield
   Do you recall what was revealed
   The day the music died
   We started singin'... bye-bye... etc.

4. And there we were all in one place, a generation lost in space
   With no time left to start again
   So come on, Jack be nimble, Jack be quick, Jack Flash sat on a candlestick
   'Cause fire is the devil's only friend
   And as I watched him on the stage my hands were clenched in fists of rage
   No angel born in hell could break that Satan's spell
   And as the flames climbed high into the night to light the sacrificial rite
   I saw Satan laughing with delight the day the music died.
   He was singin'... bye-bye... etc.

AQUALUNG

Words and Music by
IAN ANDERSON and JENNIE ANDERSON

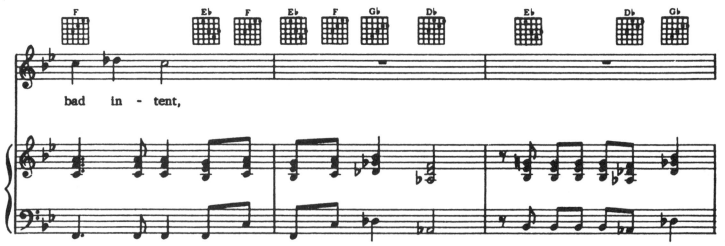

Aqualung - 6 - 1

Faster

Gm

F

Do you still re - mem - ber De -

Gm

cem - ber's fog - gy freeze when the ice that clings on -

F

Gm

to your beard was scream -ing ag - o - ny? And you

F

snatch your rat - tling last breaths with deep - sea - div - er

25

Aqualung - 6 - 6

BAD MOON RISING

Words and Music by
J.C. FOGERTY

I see the bad ____ moon a - ris - ing. ____
I hear ____ hur - ri - canes a - blow - ing. ____
Hope you ____ got your things to - geth - er. ____

I see the trou - ble on the way. ____
I know the end is com - ing soon. ____
Hope you are quite pre - pared to die. ____

I see earth - quakes and light - nin'. ____
I fear riv - ers ov - er flow - ing. ____
Looks like we're in for nas - ty weath - er. ____

Bad Moon Rising - 2 - 2

BLACK WATER

Words and Music by
PATRICK SIMMONS

Well, I built me a raft ___ and she's read - y for float - in';

ol' Mis - sis - sip pi, ___ she's call - in' my name. ___

Black Water - 6 - 1

BROWN EYED GIRL

Words and Music by
VAN MORRISON

Brown Eyed Girl - 3 - 1

36

Additional Lyrics

2. Whatever happened to Tuesday and so slow
   Going down the old mine with a transistor radio
   Standing in the sunlight laughing
   Hiding behind a rainbow's wall
   Slipping and a-sliding
   All along the water fall
   With you, my brown eyed girl
   You, my brown eyed girl.
   Do you remember when we used to sing:
   Chorus

3. So hard to find my way, now that I'm all on my own
   I saw you just the other day, my, how you have grown
   Cast my memory back there, Lord
   Sometime I'm overcome thinking 'bout
   Making love in the green grass
   Behind the stadium
   With you, my brown eyed girl
   With you, my brown eyed girl.
   Do you remember when we used to sing:
   Chorus

EUROPA
(Earth's Cry Heaven's Smile)

Music by
CARLOS SANTANA and TOM COSTER

Europa - 5 - 1

DRIVE

Words and Music by
RIC OCASEK

Who's gon - na tell you when
Who's gon - na hold you down

Drive - 8 - 1

Who's gon - na pick you up
Who's gon - na pay at - ten - tion

when you fall?
to your dreams?

46

Drive - 8 - 5

48

Drive - 8 - 7

Drive - 8 - 8

FREE BIRD

Words and Music by
ALLEN COLLINS and
RONNIE VAN ZANT

If I leave here to - mor - row,
Bye, bye ba - by it's been a sweet love

Would you still re - mem - ber
though this feel - ing I can't

me?
change.

For I must be __ trav - ling on now
But please don't take __ it so bad - ly

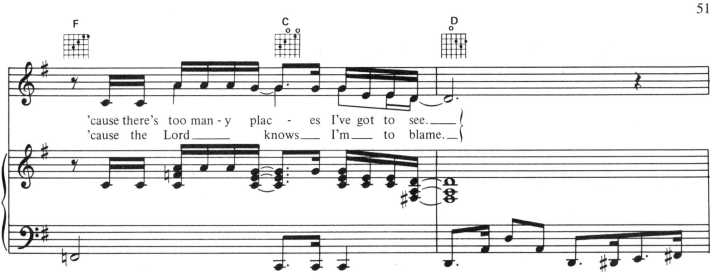

'cause there's too man - y plac - es I've got to see.___
'cause the Lord___ knows___ I'm___ to blame.___

But if I stayed here with you, girl, things just could-n't be the

same. 'Cause I'm as free___ as a bird now,

52

Free Bird - 3 - 3

GIMME SOME LOVIN'

Words and Music by
STEVE WINWOOD, MUFF WINWOOD
and SPENCER DAVIS

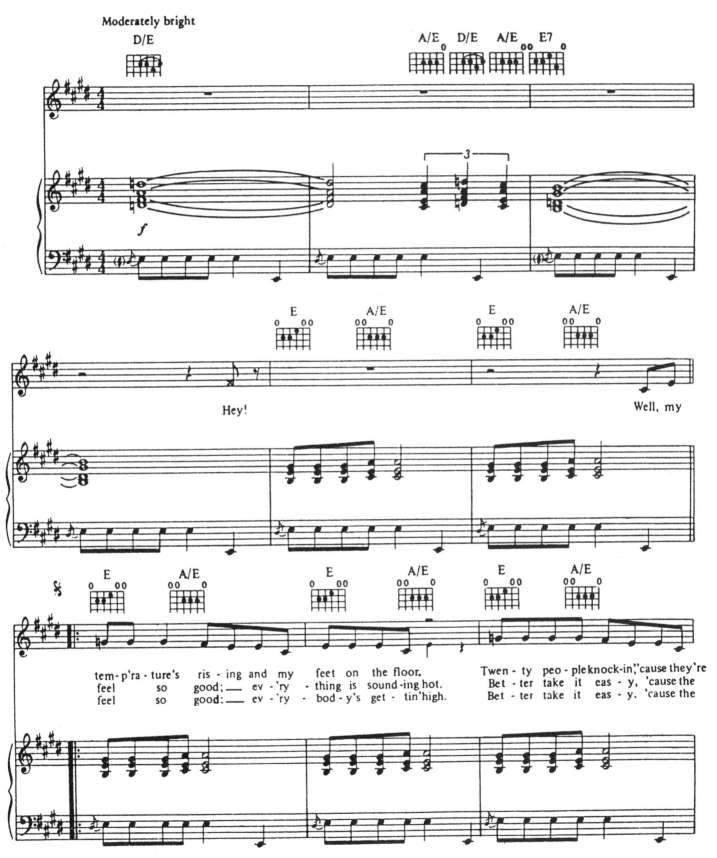

Gimme Some Lovin' - 3 - 1

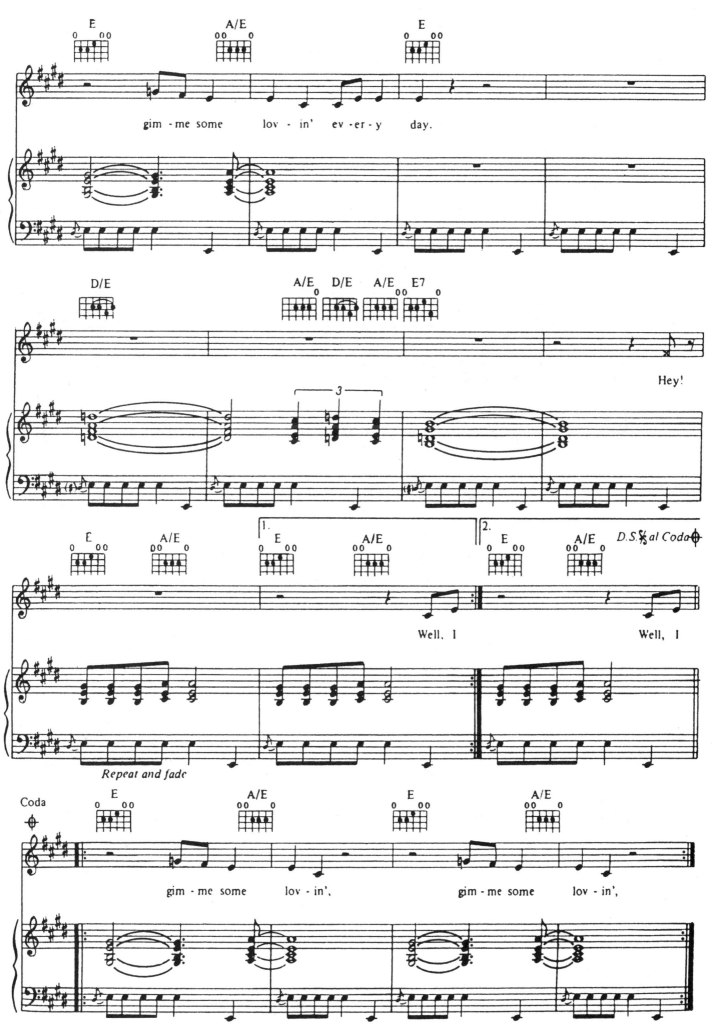

GO YOUR OWN WAY

Words and Music by
LINDSEY BUCKINGHAM

Moderately Bright Rock beat

Lov-ing you is-n't the right thing to do.
Tell me why ev-'ry-thing turned a-round.

How can I ev-er change things that I feel?
Pack-ing up, shack-ing up is all you wan-na do.

If I could, may-be I'd give you my world.
If I could, ba-by, I'd give you my world.

Go Your Own Way - 2 - 1

HEART OF GOLD

Words and Music by
NEIL YOUNG

I wan-na live, I wan-na give, I've been a min-er for a Heart Of Gold.

It's these ex-press-ions_ I nev-er give that keep me search-in' for a Heart of Gold,_____

And I'm get-tin' old. _____ Keep me search-in' for a Heart of Gold,_____

Heart of Gold - 3 - 1

59

60

Keeps me search-in' for a Heart Of Gold, _____ And I'm get-tin' old. _____

Keep me search-in' for a Heart Of Gold,__ You keep me search-in' and I'm

grow-in' old.__ Keep me search-in' for a Heart Of Gold,__

I've been a min-er for a Heart Of Gold. _____

HIGHER LOVE

Words and Music by
STEVE WINWOOD and WILL JENNINGS

62

LAYLA

Words and Music by
ERIC CLAPTON and JIM GORDON

What __ will you do when you get lone - ly?
Tried __ to give you con - so - la - tion,
Make __ the best of the sit - u - a - tion

Layla - 4 - 1

Layla - 4 - 2

68

Layla - 4 - 3

LONG TRAIN RUNNIN'

Words and Music by
TOM JOHNSTON

Long Train Runnin' - 6 - 1

72

74

Vocal Ad Lib

Got to get it, baby, baby, won't you move it down?
Won't you move it down?
Baby, baby, baby, baby, won't you move it down?
When the big train run
And the train is movin' on
I got to keep on movin',
Keep on movin',
Keep on movin',
Gonna keep on movin'.

LYIN' EYES

Words and Music by
DON HENLEY and GLENN FREY

Lyin' Eyes - 6 - 1

Lyin' Eyes - 6 - 6

MAGGIE MAY

Words and Music by
ROD STEWART and MARTIN QUITTENTON

Moderately bright

Wake up, Mag-gie, I think I got some-thing to say to you:___ It's

late Sep-tem-ber and I real-ly should be back at school. I

know I keep you a-mused,___ but I feel I'm be-ing used, Oh,

Maggie May - 3 - 1

2. You lured me away from home, just to save you from being alone.
You stole my soul, that's a pain I can do without.
All I needed was a friend to lend a guiding hand.
But you turned into a lover, and, Mother, what a lover! You wore me out.
All you did was wreck my bed, and in the morning kick me in the head.
Oh, Maggie, I couldn't have tried any more.

3. You lured me away from home, 'cause you didn't want to be alone.
You stole my heart, I couldn't leave you if I tried.
I suppose I could collect my books and get back to school.
Or steal my Daddy's cue and make a living out of playing pool,
Or find myself a rock and roll band that needs a helpin' hand.
Oh, Maggie, I wish I'd never seen your face. (To Coda)

MONEY

Words and Music by
ROGER WATERS

Mon-ey,   ya get a - way.   Ya get a
Mon-ey,   you get   back.   I'm
Mon-ey,   it's a   crime.   Share it

Money - 3 - 1

good job with more pay, and you're O. ___ K.
all right, Jack. Keep your hands off my ___ stack.
fair - ly, but don't take a slice of my ___ pie.

Mon - ey, it's a gas. Grab
Mon - ey, it's a hit. But don't
Mon - ey, so they say, is

that cash with both hands and make ___ a stash.
give me that do - good-y good bull - shit. I'm in the
the root of all e - vil to - day. But if

MORE THAN A FEELING

Words and Music by
TOM SCHOLZ

slips a - way.____

She slips a - way. _____

D.S. al Coda

Repeat
and Fade

Coda

3. When I'm tired and thinking cold
   I hide in my music, forget the day
   And dream of a girl I used to know
   I closed my eyes and she slipped away.

   (To Chorus)

OPEN ARMS

Words and Music by
STEVE PERRY and JONATHAN CAIN

1. Ly-ing____ be-side____ you, here in____ the dark; feel-ing your
2. Soft-ly____ you whis-per, you're so____ sin-cere. How could our
3.4.(see additional lyrics)

heart beat with mine.
love be so blind?____

1. We
2.(see additional lyrics)

Open Arms - 3 - 1

Verse 3:
Living without you; living alone,
This empty house seems so cold.

Verse 4:
Wanting to hold you, wanting you near;
How much I wanted you home.

Bridge:
But now that you've come back;
Turned night into day;
I need you to stay.
(Chorus)

Open Arms - 3 - 3

OLD TIME ROCK & ROLL

Words and Music by
GEORGE JACKSON and THOMAS E. JONES III

Rock and Roll tempo ♩ = 128

Just take those old re-cords

off the shelf; ___ I sit and lis - ten to them
dis - co, you'll nev - er e - ven get me

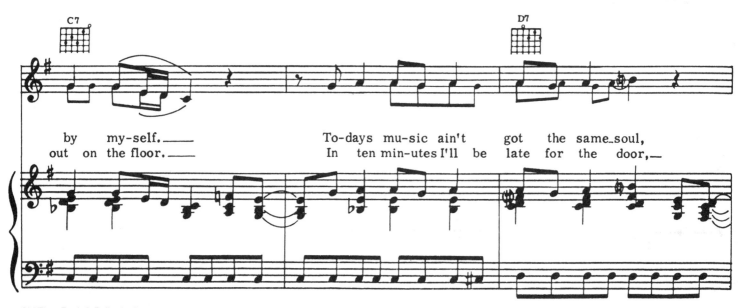

by my-self. ___ To-days mu-sic ain't got the same soul,
out on the floor. ___ In ten min-utes I'll be late for the door, ___

Old Time Rock & Roll - 4 - 1

Old Time Rock & Roll - 4 - 2

Won't go   to hear 'em play a   Still like that old___   time a

3. (Won't go to hear 'em play a) tango
   I'd rather hear some blues or funky old soul.
   There's only one sure way to get me to go
   Start playing old time rock and roll.

4. Call me a relic call me what you will
   Say I'm old-fashioned say I'm over the hill
   Today's music ain't got the same soul
   I like that old time rock and roll.

   (To Chorus)

Old Time Rock & Roll - 4 - 4

PROUD MARY

Words and Music by
J.C. FOGERTY

Proud Mary - 2 - 1

SISTER GOLDEN HAIR

Words and Music by
GERRY BECKLEY

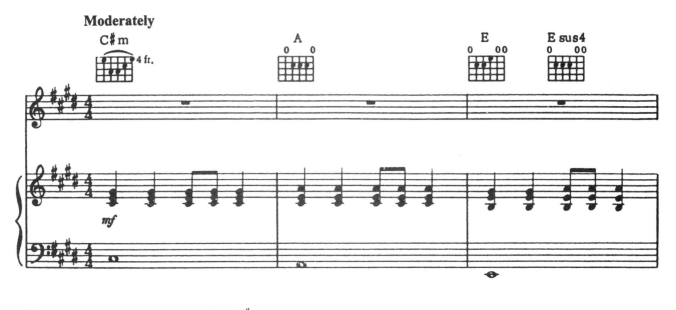

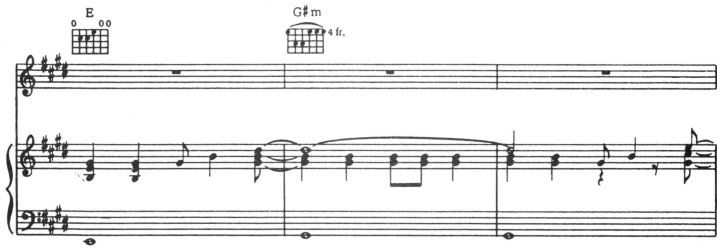

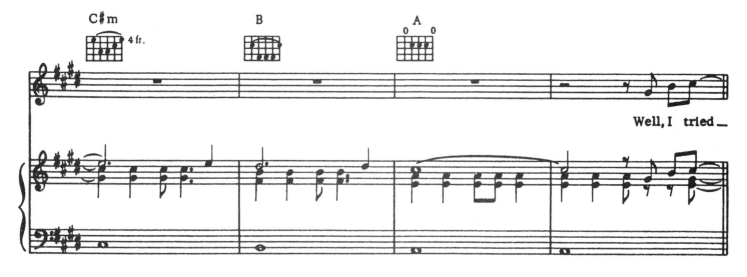

Well, I tried

Sister Golden Hair - 4 - 1

104

Sister Golden Hair - 4 - 3

TRUCKIN'

Words by
ROBERT HUNTER

Music by
JERRY GARCIA, BOB WEIR
and PHIL LESH

Truckin' - 10 - 2

108

Truckin' - 10 - 3

110

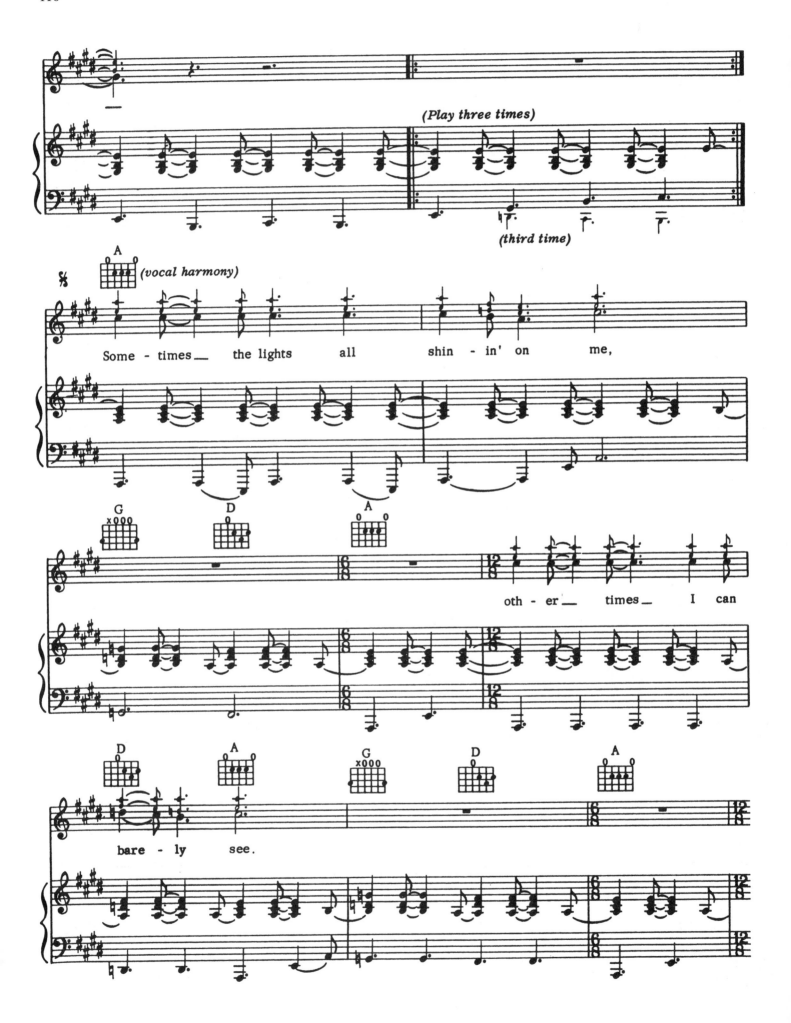

Some - times___ the lights all shin - in' on me,

oth - er___ times___ I can

bare - ly see.

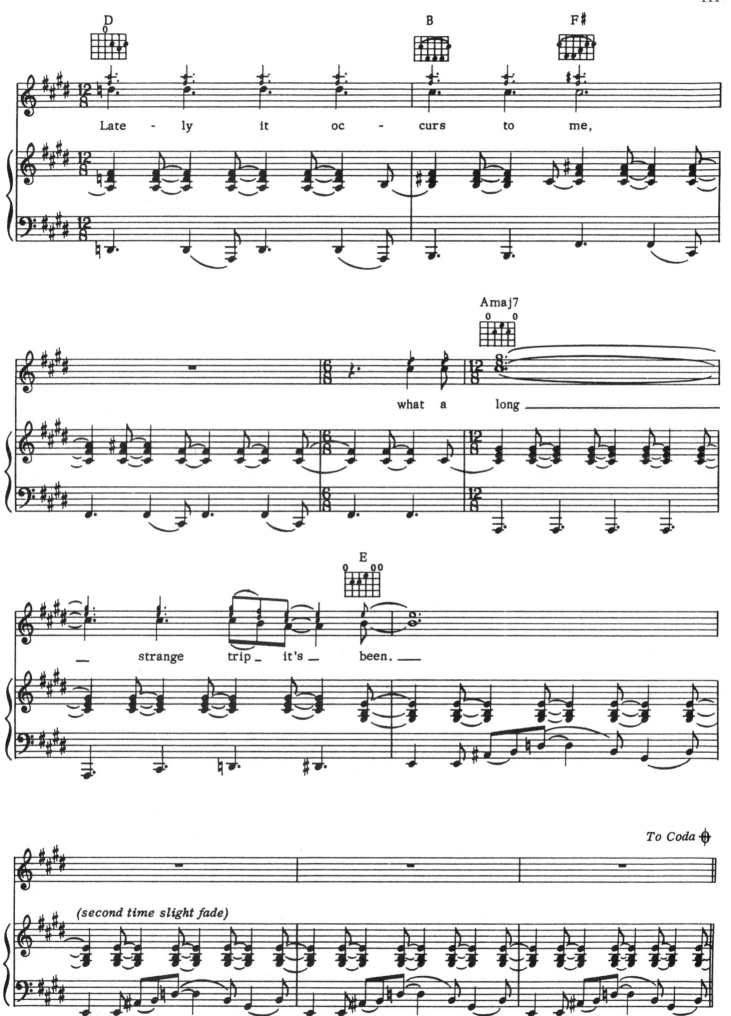

113

Truckin' - 10 - 8

You're sick of hang-in' a-round, and you'd like to trav - el.___ Get

tired___ of trav-el-lin', you want to set-tle down.___ I

guess they can't re-voke___ your soul for try - in',___ get

D. S. ℟ al Coda ⊕

out of the door, light out and look all a - round.___

SOMEONE SAVED MY LIFE TONIGHT

Words and Music by
ELTON JOHN and BERNIE TAUPIN

Someone Saved My Life Tonight - 5 - 1

D.S. al Coda 𝄋

save your strength__ and run the field you play a - lone.__

Some-one saved, some-one saved, some-one saved my life__ to - night.__

ADDITIONAL LYRICS

Verse 2.

I never realised the passing hours
Of evening showers,
A slip noose hanging in my darkest dreams.
I'm strangled by your haunted social scene
Just a pawn out - played by a dominating queen.
It's four - o - clock in the morning
Damn it!
Listen to me good.
I'm sleeping with myself tonight
Saved in time, thank God my music's still alive.

To Chorus.

WHAT A FOOL BELIEVES

Words and Music by
KENNY LOGGINS and MICHAEL McDONALD

What a Fool Believes - 5 - 1

122

What a Fool Believes - 5 - 2

123

What a Fool Believes - 5 - 3

124

What a Fool Believes - 5 - 4

DOWN ON THE CORNER

Words and Music by
JOHN C. FOGERTY

100 years of Popular Music

Celebrate All the Classic Hits of the 20th Century with This New Series from Warner Bros. Publications

Eighty-nine hits from 1900 to 1920 in one collection! Aba Daba Honeymoon • Alexander's Ragtime Band • The Band Played On • A Bicycle Built for Two • Bill Bailey, Won't You Please Come Home? • Danny Boy • The Entertainer • Give My Regards to Broadway • Meet Me in St. Louis, Louis • Over There • Take Me Out to the Ball Game • When Irish Eyes Are Smiling • When the Saints Go Marching In • You're a Grand Old Flag, and many more.

1900 (MFM0306)

More than 250 pages of classic songs from the Roaring Twenties! Ain't We Got Fun • The Birth of the Blues • Bye Bye Blackbird • The Charleston • Clap Yo' Hands • Fascinating Rhythm • Get Happy • Hard-Hearted Hannah • I'm Just Wild About Harry • Ma! (He's Making Eyes at Me) • Makin' Whoopee! • Ol' Man River • 'S Wonderful • Singin' in the Rain • The Varsity Drag, and many more.

1920 (MFM0307)

A smokin' collection of favorites from the thirties! Ain't Misbehavin' • A-Tisket, A-Tasket • Begin the Beguine • Bei Mir Bist Du Schön • Embraceable You • A Fine Romance • Forty-Second Street • Hooray for Hollywood • I Got Rhythm • I've Got a Crush on You • Jeepers Creepers • Let's Call the Whole Thing Off • Lullaby of Broadway • My Heart Belongs to Daddy • Over the Rainbow • Summertime • The Way You Look Tonight, and many more.

1930 (MFM0308)

From the swingin' forties comes this incredible collection! Beat Me Daddy, Eight to the Bar • Bewitched • Body and Soul • Boogie Woogie Bugle Boy • Chattanooga Choo Choo • How High the Moon • I've Got a Gal in Kalamazoo • New York, New York • On Green Dolphin Street • Pennsylvania 6-5000 • 'Round Midnight • You Make Me Feel So Young, and many more.

1940 (MFM0309)

Catch all the smooth stylings and rock 'n' roll of the fifties! Blue Suede Shoes • Catch a Falling Star • Chances Are • Earth Angel • Enchanted • Good Golly Miss Molly • Great Balls of Fire • Mack the Knife • Only You (And You Alone) • Que Sera, Sera • (We're Gonna) Rock Around the Clock • Smoke Gets in Your Eyes • Splish Splash • Tammy • The Twelfth of Never, and many more.

1950 (MFM0310)

Collect all the soulful tunes of the sixties! Be My Baby • Brown-Eyed Girl • California Dreamin' • Chain of Fools • Crying • The Girl from Ipanema • I Say a Little Prayer • I Want to Hold Your Hand • It's Not Unusual • Let's Twist Again • Na Na Hey Hey Kiss Him Goodbye • Oh, Pretty Woman • Poetry in Motion • Proud Mary, and many more.

1960 (MFM0311)

Rock out with these great tunes from the seventies! All by Myself • American Pie • Can't Get Enough of Your Love, Babe • Dancing Queen • I Will Survive • If You Love Me (Let Me Know) • Killing Me Softly with His Song • Old Time Rock & Roll • Sister Golden Hair • Sweet Home Alabama • You're So Vain, and many more.

1970 (MFM0312)

All the unforgettable hits of the Me Decade! 1-2-3 • Addicted to Love • Arthur's Theme • Beat It • Call Me • Maneater • Morning Train (Nine to Five) • Owner of a Lonely Heart • The Safety Dance • She Works Hard for the Money • That's What Friends Are For • What's Love Got to Do with It • We Built This City • You Give Love a Bad Name, and many more.

1980 (MFM0313)

The hottest hits of the last decade! All for Love • All I Wanna Do • Believe • Dreaming of You • From This Moment On • Have I Told You Lately • Hold On • How Do I Live • I Will Always Love You • Insensitive • Ironic • Livin' la Vida Loca • Macarena • Save the Best for Last • Smooth • Stay (I Missed You) • Un-Break My Heart • Waiting for Tonight • Where Does My Heart Beat Now, and many more.

1990 (MFM0314)

All the modern hits of the new millennium so far! Bye Bye Bye • Can't Get You Out of My Head • Come on Over (All I Want Is You) • Complicated • Cry Me a River • Dilemma • Everywhere • Hero • Hey Baby • I'm Like a Bird • Love Don't Cost a Thing • Music • Show Me the Meaning of Being Lonely • Thank You • A Thousand Miles, and many more.

2000 (MFM0315)

All editions are arranged for Piano/Vocal/Chords

AD1116 07/03